A-Z Animal Coloring & Activity Book

ENGLISH & SPANISH

Kevin Hill

authorHOUSE®

AuthorHouse™
1663 Liberty Drive
Bloomington, IN 47403
www.authorhouse.com
Phone: 1-800-839-8640

Published by AuthorHouse   05/08/2012

ISBN: 978-1-4772-0407-8 (sc)
ISBN: 978-1-4772-0406-1 (e)

This book is printed on acid-free paper.

DRAW YOUR OWN PICTURE OF THE ANIMAL HERE.

ALLIGATOR   CAIMÁN

A

DRAW YOUR OWN PICTURE OF THE ANIMAL HERE.

BEAR   OSO

B

DRAW YOUR OWN PICTURE OF THE ANIMAL HERE.

CAMEL

CAMELLO

C

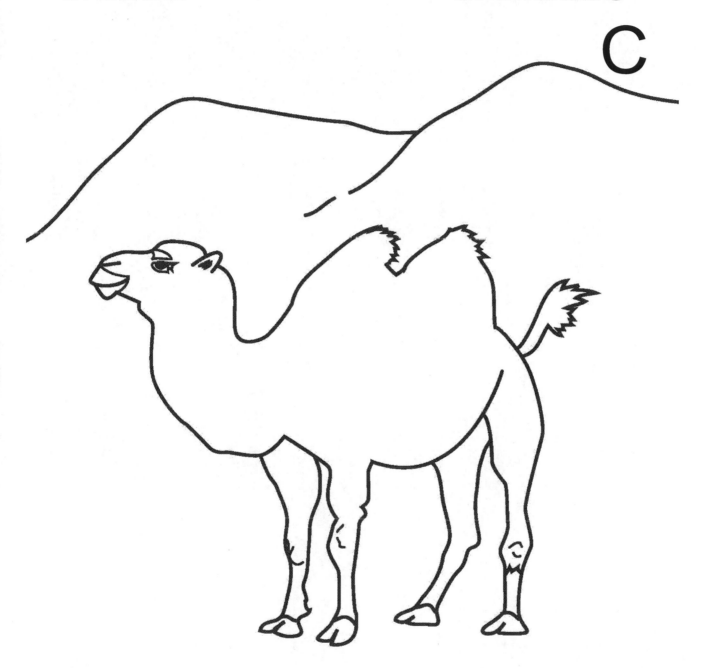

DRAW YOUR OWN PICTURE OF THE ANIMAL HERE.

DOG

PERRO

D

DRAW YOUR OWN PICTURE OF THE ANIMAL HERE.

ELEPHANT

ELEFANTE

E

DRAW YOUR OWN PICTURE OF THE ANIMAL HERE.

FROG

RANA

F

DRAW YOUR OWN PICTURE OF THE ANIMAL HERE.

GOAT

CHIVO

G

DRAW YOUR OWN PICTURE OF THE ANIMAL HERE.

HORSE

CABALLO

H

DRAW YOUR OWN PICTURE OF THE ANIMAL HERE.

IGUANA

IGUANA

I

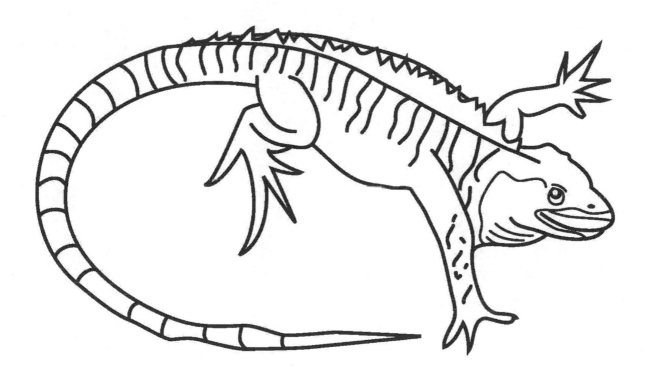

DRAW YOUR OWN PICTURE OF THE ANIMAL HERE.

JAGUAR

JAGUAR

J

DRAW YOUR OWN PICTURE OF THE ANIMAL HERE.

KANGAROO

CANGURO

K

DRAW YOUR OWN PICTURE OF THE ANIMAL HERE.

LION

LEÓN

L

DRAW YOUR OWN PICTURE OF THE ANIMAL HERE.

MONKEY

MONO

M

DRAW YOUR OWN PICTURE OF THE ANIMAL HERE.

NEWT

TRITÓN

N

DRAW YOUR OWN PICTURE OF THE ANIMAL HERE.

OWL BÚHO

O

DRAW YOUR OWN PICTURE OF THE ANIMAL HERE.

PENGUIN

PINGUINO

P

DRAW YOUR OWN PICTURE OF THE ANIMAL HERE.

QUAIL   CODORNIZ
Q

DRAW YOUR OWN PICTURE OF THE ANIMAL HERE.

RABBIT

CONEJO

R

DRAW YOUR OWN PICTURE OF THE ANIMAL HERE.

SEAL

FOCA

S

DRAW YOUR OWN PICTURE OF THE ANIMAL HERE.

TURTLE

TORTUGA

T

DRAW YOUR OWN PICTURE OF THE ANIMAL HERE.

UNICORN

UNICORNIO

U

DRAW YOUR OWN PICTURE OF THE ANIMAL HERE.

VIPER

VIBORA

V

DRAW YOUR OWN PICTURE OF THE ANIMAL HERE.

WHALE

BALLENA

W

DRAW YOUR OWN PICTURE OF THE ANIMAL HERE.

XRAY FISH

XRAY PESCADO

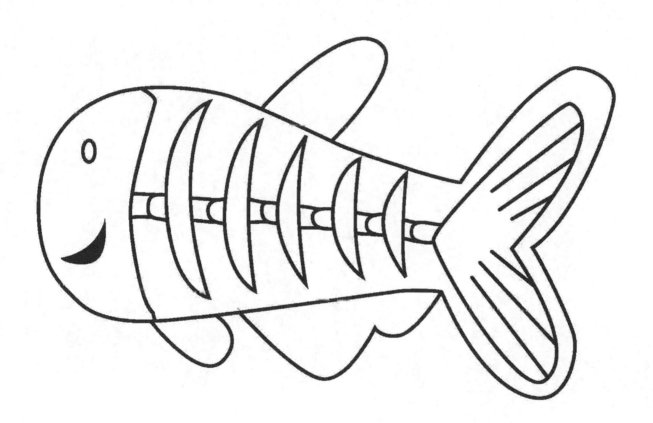

DRAW YOUR OWN PICTURE OF THE ANIMAL HERE.

YAK   YAC

Y

DRAW YOUR OWN PICTURE OF THE ANIMAL HERE.

ZEBRA   CEBRA

Z

Printed in the United States
By Bookmasters